The Comedy Songs of
GEORGE & IRA GERSHWIN

Project Manager: Tony Esposito
Book Art Layout: Odalis Soto

GEORGE & IRA GERSHWIN

George Gershwin, born in Brooklyn, New York on September 26, 1898, began his musical training at thirteen. At fifteen he left high school to work as a Tin Pan Alley "song plugger" and within three years he had seen his first song published. Although "When You Want 'Em You Cant't Get 'Em, When You've Got 'Em You Don't Want 'Em" created little interest, George's "Swanee," popularized by Al Jolson in 1919, brought Gershwin his first real fame. In 1924, when George teamed up with his older brother Ira, "the Gershwins" became the dominant Broadway songwriters, creating brisk, infectious rhythm numbers and affectingly poignant ballads, invariably fashioning the words to fit the melodies with a "glove-like" fidelity. This extraordinary collaboration led to a succession of musical comedies, among them *Lady, Be Good!* (1924), *Oh, Kay!* (1926), *Funny Face* (1927), *Strike Up the Band* (1927 & 1930), *Girl Crazy* (1930), and *Of Thee I Sing* (1931), the first musical comedy to win a Pulitzer Prize. Over the years, Gershwin songs have also been used in numerous films including *Shall We Dance* (1937), *A Damsel in Distress* (1937) and *An American in Paris* (1951). Later years produced the award-winning stage musicals *My One and Only* (1983) and *Crazy for You* (1992) which ran four years on Broadway.

Starting with his early days as a composer of songs, Gershwin had ambitions to compose serious music. Asked by Paul Whiteman to write an original work for a special modern concert to be presented at Aeolian Hall in New York on February 12, 1924, Gershwin, who was hard at work on a musical comedy, *Sweet Little Devil*, barely completed his composition in time. Commencing with the first low trill of the solo clarinet and its spine-tingling run up the scale, *Rhapsody in Blue* caught the public's fancy and opened a new era in American music. In 1925, the eminent conductor Walter Damrosch commissioned Gershwin to compose a piano concerto for the New York Symphony Society. Many feel that the *Concerto in F* is Gershwin's finest orchestral work. Others opt for his *An American in Paris* (1928) or his *Second Rhapsody* for piano and orchestra, which he introduced with himself as pianist with the Boston Symphony under Serge Koussevitzky in 1932.

In 1926 Gershwin came across DuBose Heyward's novel *Porgy*, and immediately recognized it as a perfect vehicle for a "folk opera" using blues and jazz idioms. *Porgy and Bess* (co-written with DuBose and Dorothy Heyward and Ira Gershwin) was the Gershwin brothers' most ambitious undertaking, tightly integrating unforgettable songs with dramatic incident. *Porgy and Bess* previewed in Boston beginning September 30, 1935, and opened its Broadway run on October 10th. The opera had major revivals in 1942, 1952, 1976 and 1983 and toured the world. It was made into a major motion picture by Samuel Goldwyn in 1959. Trevor Nunn's landmark Glyndeboune Opera production was taped for television in 1993.

In 1937, George Gershwin was at the height of his career. His symphonic works and three *Preludes for Piano* were becoming part of the standard repertoire for concerts and recitals, and his show songs had brought him ever-increasing fame and fortune. It was in Hollywood, while he was working on the score of *The Goldwyn Follies*, that George Gershwin collapsed and died of a brain tumor; he was not quite 39 years old. Countless people throughout the world, who knew Gershwin only through his work, were stunned by the news as if they had suffered a personal loss. Some years later, John O'Hara summed up the feelings that abide: "George Gershwin died July 11, 1937, but I don't have to believe it if I don't want to."

Today Gershwin's works are performed with greater frequency than they were during his brief lifetime. The songs and concert pieces are not in the least ephemeral, as a glance at the pages of any record catalogue will quickly make evident. Certainly the Trustees of Columbia University must have recognized this when they awarded George Gershwin a special posthumous Pulitzer Prize in 1998, the centennial of his birth.

Ira Gershwin, the first lyricist to be awarded a Pulitzer Prize — *Of Thee I Sing*, 1932 — was born in New York City on December 6, 1896. (His brother, George, with whom he was to make of *Gershwin* a hallmark for distinguished musical-comedy songs, was born twenty-one months later in Brooklyn.) While attending the College of the City of New York, Ira began demonstrating his lifelong interest in light verse and contributed droll quatrains and squibs to newspaper columnists. In 1918 while working as the desk attendant in a Turkish bath, he tentatively began a collaboration with his brother, and their "The Real American Folk Song (Is a Rag)" was heard in Nora Bayes's *Ladies First*. Not wanting to trade on the success of his already famous brother, Ira soon afterward adopted the nom de plume of Arthur Francis, combining the names of his youngest brother Arthur and sister Frances. Under this pen name in 1921 Ira supplied lyrics for his first Broadway show, *Two Little Girls in Blue*, with music by another newcomer, Vincent Youmans.

After writing songs for three more years with a variety of composers, Ira was ready in 1924 to begin the successful and lifelong collaboration with George and dropped the pseudonym. Thus it was as the "Gershwin Brothers" that George and Ira created the hit, *Lady, Be Good!*, featuring Fred and Adele Astaire, the first of the Gershwins' more than twenty scores for stage and screen, including *Oh, Kay!* for Gertrude Laurence; two versions of *Strike Up the Band* (1927 & 1930); Ethel Merman's introduction to Broadway, *Girl Crazy* (1930); *Shall We Dance* (1937), one of Hollywood's stylish pairings of Fred Astaire and Ginger Rogers; and the triumphant opera, *Porgy and Bess*, written with DuBose Heyward. Before and after George's death in 1937 Ira also collaborated with such composers as Harold Arlen (*A Star Is Born*, 1954), Vernon Duke (*The Ziegfeld Follies of 1936*), Kurt Weill (*Lady in the Dark*, 1941), Jerome Kern (*Cover Girl*, 1944), Harry Warren (*The Barkleys of Broadway*, 1949, the final Astaire/Rogers picture), Arthur Schwartz (*Park Avenue*, 1946), and Burton Lane (*Give a Girl a Break*, 1953).

For his achievements in film scores Ira Gershwin was nominated three times for an Academy Award for the songs "They Can't Take That Away From Me," "Long Ago (and Far Away)" (his biggest song hit in any one year) and "The Man That Got Away." In 1966 he received a Doctor of Fine Arts degree from the University of Maryland, confirming the judgment of so many of his literary admirers — writers like Dashiell Hammett, Lillian Hellman, Dorothy Parker, S.N. Behrman, P.G. Wodehouse, W.H. Auden, Ogden Nash, and Larry Hart, to name only a few — that his work was not only of the first rank, but that the Gershwin "standards" set new standards for the American musical theatre. Small wonder that the Gershwin *oeuvre* has been taken up enthusiastically by a younger generation who have delighted in the "new" Gershwin musicals, *My One and Only* (1983) and the 1992 Tony Award winner for best musical, *Crazy for You*.

In all the years after George's death, Ira assiduously attended to the Gershwin legacy of songs, show and film scores, and concert works. Ira annotated all the materials that pertain to the careers of his brother and himself before donating them to the Library of Congress to become a part of our national heritage. In 1985 the United States Congress recognized this legacy by awarding the Congressional Gold Medal to George and Ira Gershwin, only the third time in our nation's history that songwriters had been so honored. On August 17, 1983, Ira Gershwin died peacefully in the "Gershwin Plantation," the Beverly Hills home that since 1940 he had shared with Leonore, his wife of 56 years, to whom he had dedicated his unique compendium of lyrics, musings, observations, and anecdotes: the critically acclaimed *Lyrics on Several Occasions* (1959, 1997).

FOREWORD

George and Ira Gershwin gave us some of the most beautiful and swinging songs ever written for the Broadway stage. We're transported back in time when we hear the familiar strains of such classics as "Fascinatin' Rhythm," "I Got Rhythm," "The Man I love," "Someone to Watch Over Me," "How Long Has This Been Going On?" "Of Thee I Sing," "'S Wonderful" and "Embraceable You." These songs, which were featured in the Gershwins' shows, helped establish characters' parts and define plots.

The songs featured in this folio played the same role in their respective shows, but they also added the element of comedy. The genius team that gave us the songs listed above also wrote "Blah-Blah-Blah," "Could You Use Me," "I Want to Be a War Bride," "I Won't Say I Will, but I Won't Say I Won't," "I'm a Poached Egg," "Stiff Upper Lip," "Naughty Baby," "The Jolly Tar and the Milkmaid," "Just Another Rhumba," "The Babbitt and the Bromide" and "Sam & Delilah." This songbook celebrates these and many other delightful comedy tunes penned by the brothers Gershwin.

If you love theater music, you'll love this folio. If you perform theater music, you'll love this folio. If you love and admire the songs of George and Ira Gershwin, we know you'll love this folio!

CONTENTS

THE BABBITT AND THE BROMIDE

Music and Lyrics by
GEORGE GERSHWIN and IRA GERSHWIN

The Babbitt and the Bromide - 5 - 1

No Chord   F#7

They both were sol - id cit - i - zens they
That they had both de - vel -oped in ten
A harp each one was car - ry - ing and

Eb7   F#7

both had been a - round, And as they spoke you clear - ly saw their
years, there was no doubt, And so, of course, they had an aw - ful
both were wear - ing wings, And this is what they said as they were

A7   N.C.

feet were on the ground.
lot to talk a - bout;
strum-ming on the strings;

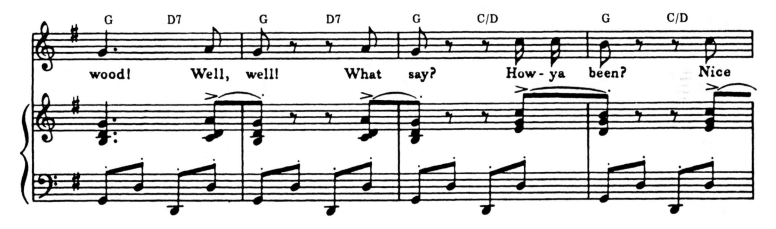

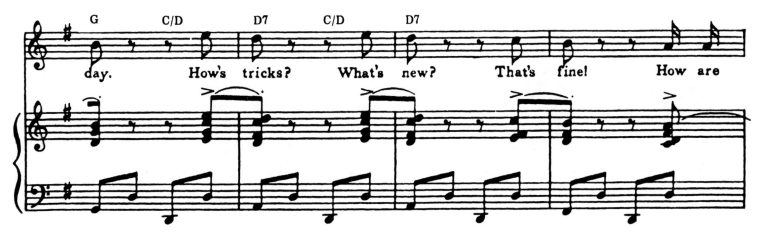

The Babbitt and the Bromide - 5 - 3

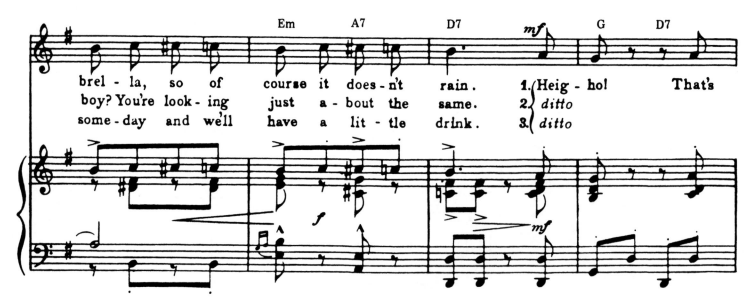

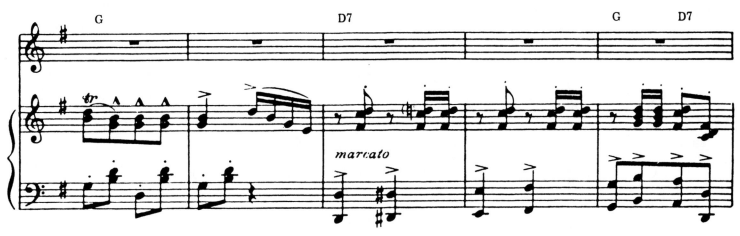

The Babbitt and the Bromide - 5 - 5

BLAH-BLAH-BLAH

Music and Lyrics by
GEORGE GERSHWIN and IRA GERSHWIN

Blah-Blah-Blah - 4 - 1

learned it from the screen. (I hope you like it)_____ I

stud-ied all the rhymes that all the lov-ers sing;_____ Then

just for you I wrote this lit-tle thing._____

Refrain

Blah, blah, blah, blah moon,   Blah, blah, blah a - bove,

Blah-Blah-Blah - 4 - 2

12

BOY! WHAT LOVE HAS DONE TO ME!

Music and Lyrics by
GEORGE GERSHWIN and IRA GERSHWIN

Boy! What Love Has Done to Me! - 5 - 1

Am7   D7   G   Em7   D   G   G7

af - ter.   Of   mil - lion - aires   she   had   her   pick,___   but   she

Cmaj7   C   Eb+   Cm   Bb+   D7   Em7   C#dim   Cm6   Bm   D7   G

played her - self   a   dir - ty   trick___   when   she   chose   that   guy   whose   name   is   Slick.___   She's a

Em   Em7   Am7   D7   Em   Em7   A7   D7

rit.

sap   to   love   him   so;   lis - ten   to   her   tale   of   woe:

rit.

Rather slow *(sorrowfully)*

Refrain:

G   *poco a poco cresc.*   G#dim   Am6   3   C#dim

p - mf

1. I   fetch   his   slip - pers;   fill   up   the   pipe   he   smokes.   I   cook   the   kip - pers;
2. *See additional lyrics*

p - mf   *poco a poco cresc.*

16

Boy! What Love Has Done to Me! - 5 - 4

18

I got a wed-ding ring; and still I love him, there's no-bod-y a-bove him!

Boy! What love has done to me! me!

Second Refrain:
His brains are minus,
Never a thought in sight—
And yet his highness
Lectures me day and night;
Oh, where was my sense
To sign that wedding license?
Boy! What love had done to me!

My life he's wrecking;
Bet you could find him now
Out somewhere necking
Somebody else's frau.
You get to know life
When married to a low-life—
Boy! What love has done to me!

I can't hold my head up:
The butcher, the baker,
All know he's a faker;
Brother, I am fed up—
But if I left him he'd be up a tree.

Where will I wind up?
I don't know where I'm at.
I make my mind up
I ought to leave him flat.
But I have grown so
I love the dirty so'n'so!
Boy! What love has done to me!

BY STRAUSS

Music and Lyrics by
GEORGE GERSHWIN and IRA GERSHWIN

Tempo di Valse Viennoise

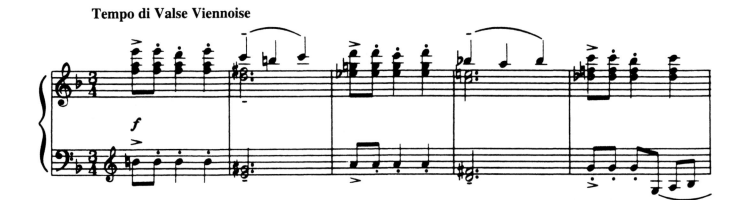

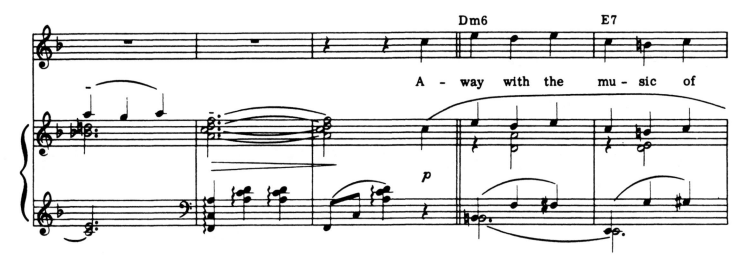

A - way with the mu - sic of

Broad- way! _____ Be off with your Irv - ing Ber - lin! _____

By Strauss - 5 - 1

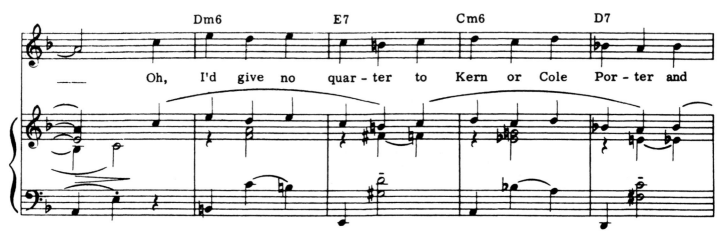

Oh, I'd give no quar - ter to Kern or Cole Por - ter and

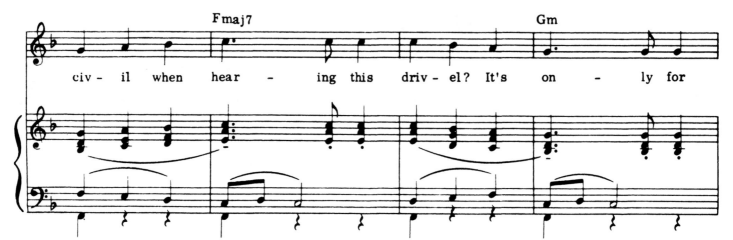

Gersh-win keeps pound-ing on tin._____ How can I be

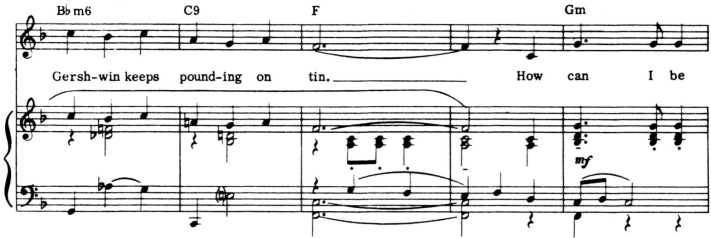

civ - il when hear - ing this driv - el? It's on - ly for

night club-bing sous - es._____ Oh, give me the free 'n' eas - y

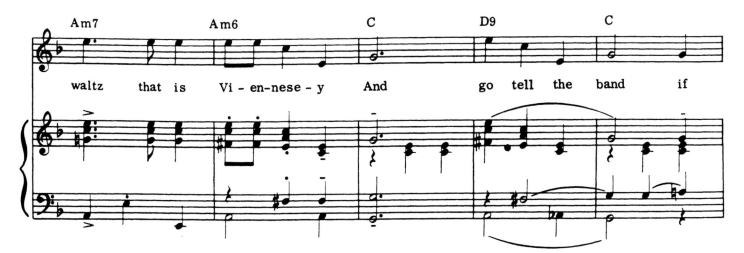

waltz that is Vi-en-nese-y And go tell the band if

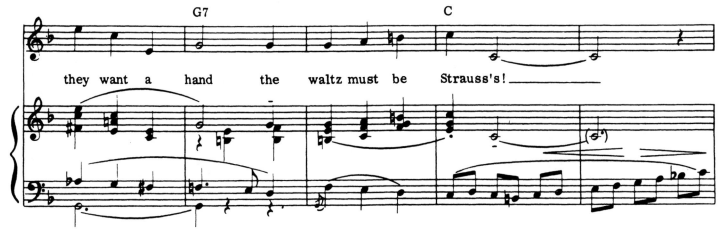

they want a hand the waltz must be Strauss's! _____

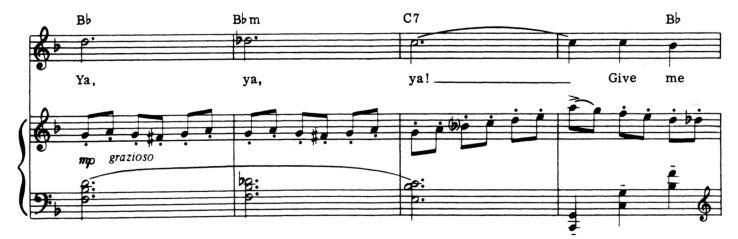

Ya, ya, ya! _____ Give me

oom - pah - pah! _____

22

By Strauss - 5 - 4

COULD YOU USE ME?

Music and Lyrics by
GEORGE GERSHWIN and IRA GERSHWIN

Could You Use Me? - 4 - 1

-ply-ing for, / -for-ni - a — Let me put it to you thus: / More ro-man-tic far than you. — It's a part-ner-ship I'm / When he sings "Ha-Cha-Cha-

dy - ing for / Chor-ni - a" — Mis - ter and Mis - sis / I oft-en think he'll — Us! / do. — Be - fore you file it / But as for you, Sir,

on the shelf / I'm a-fraid you will — Let me tell you of my - self. / nev - er make the grade. — Oh, / For,

REFRAIN

Danny: I'm the chap-pie, To make you hap-py. I'll tie your shoes-ies And
Ginger: You're no cow-boy; You're soft and how!_ boy! I feel no mus-cle, That's

I'm no Elk or Mas-on or Wood-man, Who gets home at three. The
Could you warm me up in a bliz-zard, Say, for-ty be-low? Your

girls who see— me Grow soft and dream-y, But I'm a gan-der who
ties are freak-ish; Your knees look weak-ish, Go back to flap-pers And

won't phil-an-der, Oh, could you use— me? Cause I cer-tain-ly could use
high-ball lap-pers! Though you can use— me, I most cer-tain-ly can't use

you!_____ Oh, you!_____
For,

SAM AND DELILAH

Music and Lyrics by
GEORGE GERSHWIN and IRA GERSHWIN

Tempo di Blues

Sam and Delilah - 6 - 1

De - li - lah_____ was-n't choos-ey_____ till she

fell for a swell buck-a-roo whose name was Sam._____

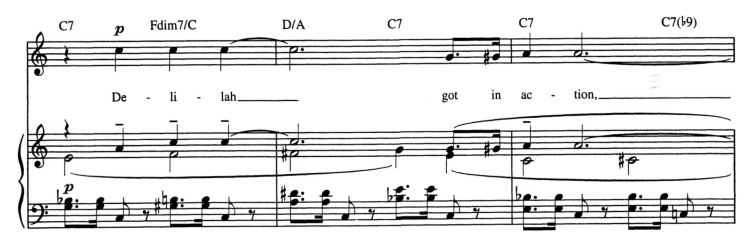

De - li - lah_____ got in ac - tion,_____

De - li - lah_____ did her

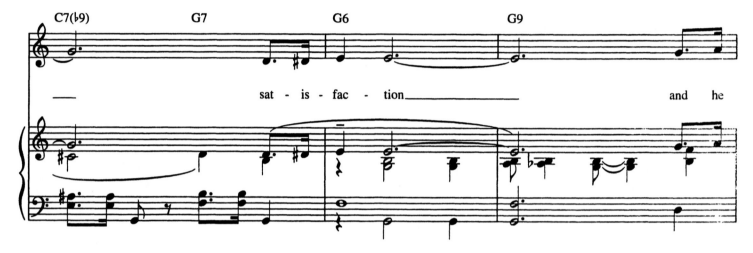

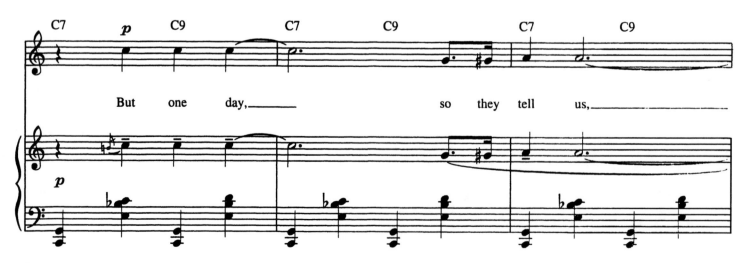

Sam and Delilah - 6 - 3

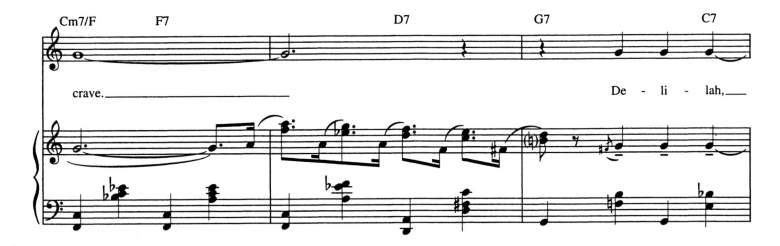

It's al-ways that way with pas-sion, so cow-boy, learn to be-

have, or else you're li-'ble to cash in

with no tomb-stone on your grave.

Broad *Kate and ensemble*

De-li-lah,___ oh! De-li-lah,___

ben marcato

Sam and Delilah - 6 - 6

I MUST BE HOME BY TWELVE O'CLOCK

Music and Lyrics by
GEORGE GERSHWIN, IRA GERSHWIN
and GUS KAHN

I Must Be Home by Twelve O'clock - 4 - 1

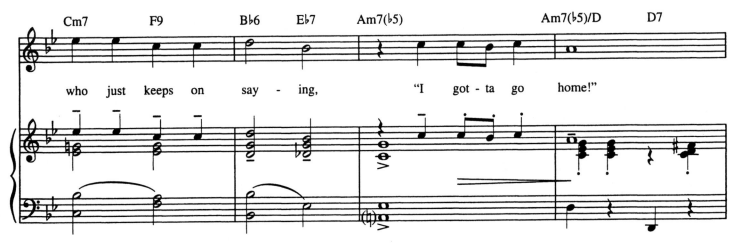

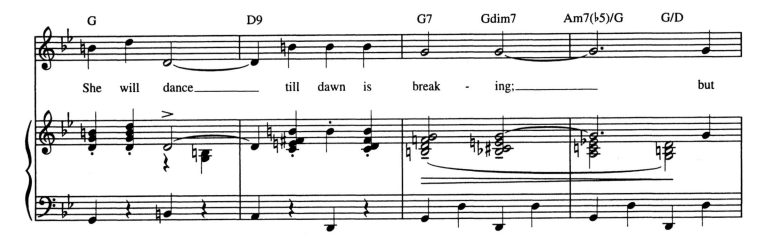

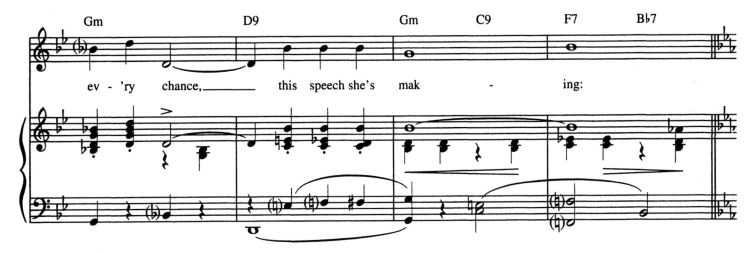

I Must Be Home by Twelve O'clock - 4 - 2

I Must Be Home by Twelve O'clock - 4 - 4

I WANT TO BE A WAR BRIDE

Music and Lyrics by
GEORGE GERSHWIN and IRA GERSHWIN

I Want to Be a War Bride - 4 - 1

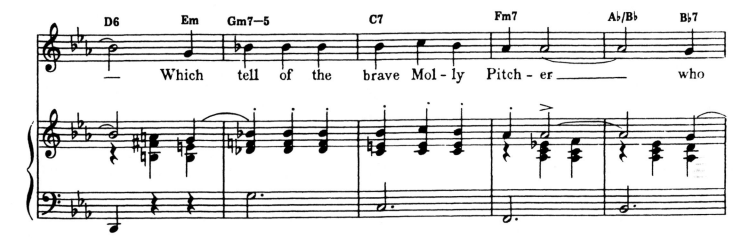

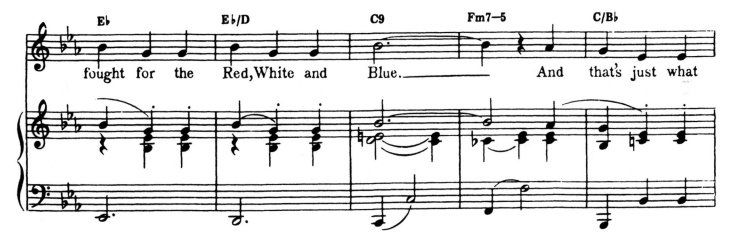

I Want to Be a War Bride - 4 - 2

Here I am, Will ing to suf-fer for you.____

Refrain

I've an i - de - a, I want to be a blush-ing,

blush-ing war bride.____ Oh, to be rapt in

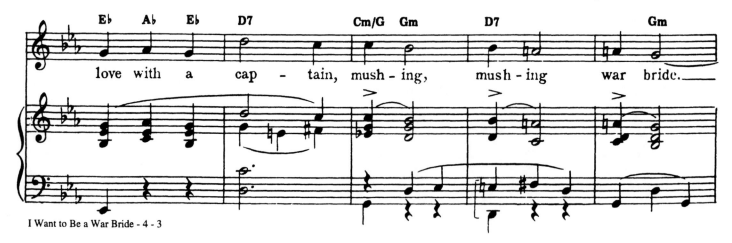

love with a cap - tain, mush-ing, mush-ing war bride.____

I Want to Be a War Bride - 4 - 3

If he's a colo-nel I'll prom-ise love e-ter-nal; to a

ma-jor I can wa-ger to be true;_____ Ev-en a

pri-vate still could con-trive it to make me a war bride.

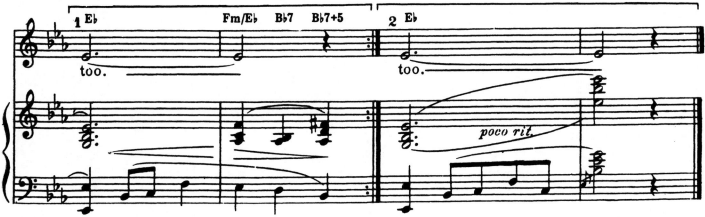

too._____   too._____

I Want to Be a War Bride - 4 - 4

I WON'T SAY I WILL,
BUT I WON'T SAY I WON'T

Lyrics by
B.G. DeSYLVA and
ARTHUR FRANCIS *(Ira Gershwin)*

Music by
GEORGE GERSHWIN

I Won't Say I Will, But I Won't Say I Won't - 5 - 1

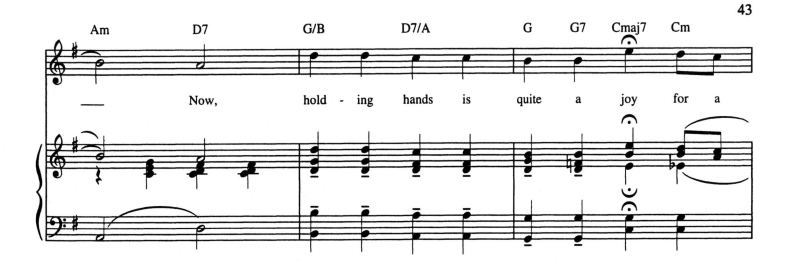

Now, hold - ing hands is quite a joy for a

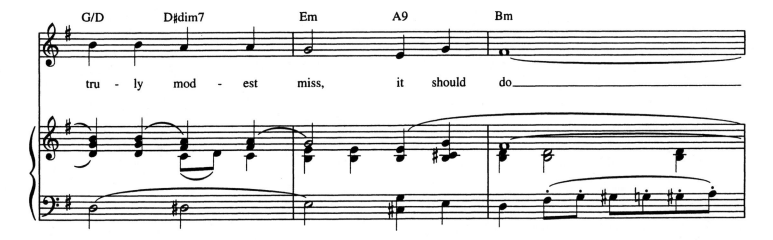

tru - ly mod - est miss, it should do_____

just as well for you,_____ I am

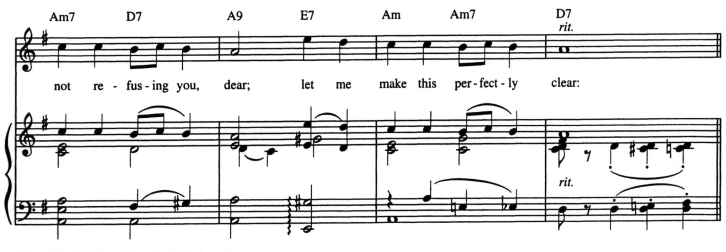

not re - fus - ing you, dear; let me make this per - fect - ly clear:

I Won't Say I Will, But I Won't Say I Won't - 5 - 2

44

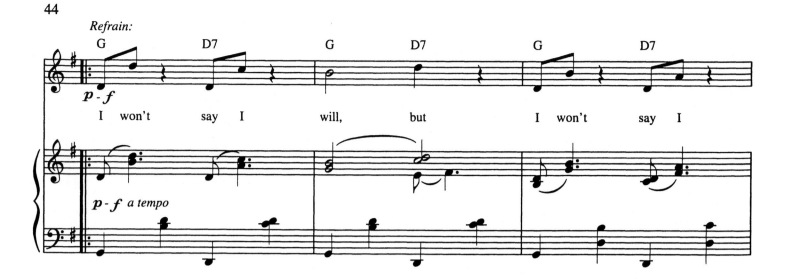

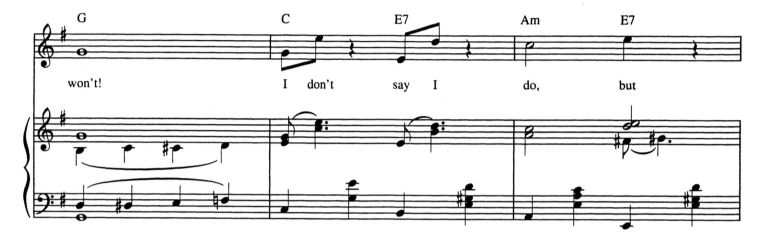

I Won't Say I Will, But I Won't Say I Won't - 5 - 3

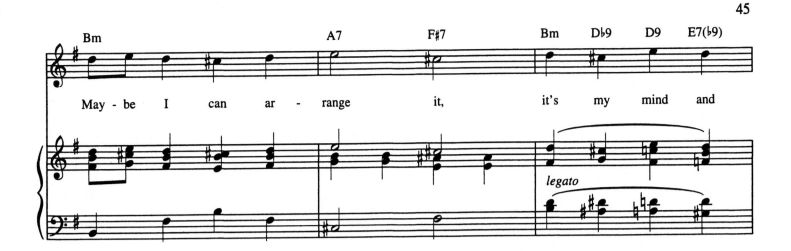

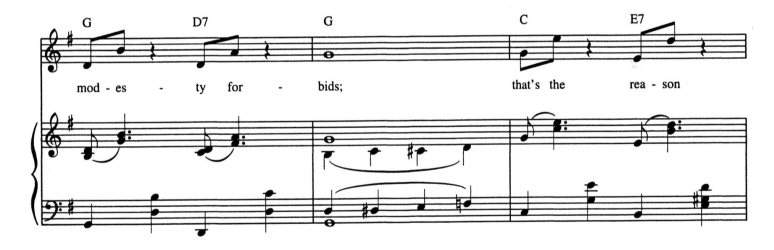

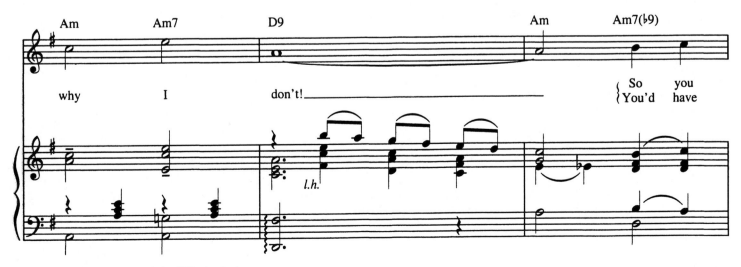

I Won't Say I Will, But I Won't Say I Won't - 5 - 4

I Won't Say I Will, But I Won't Say I Won't - 5 - 5

THE ILLEGITIMATE DAUGHTER

Music and Lyrics by
GEORGE GERSHWIN and IRA GERSHWIN

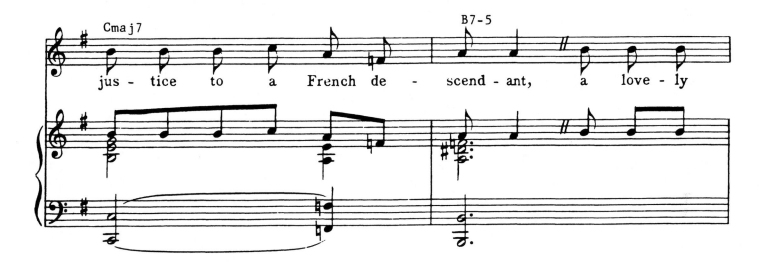

(French Ambassador to the President)

You have done a great in-

jus - tice to a French de - scend - ant, a love - ly

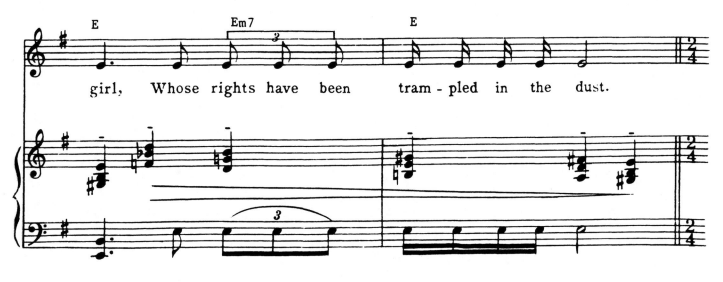

girl, Whose rights have been tram - pled in the dust.

The Illegitimate Daughter - 5 - 1

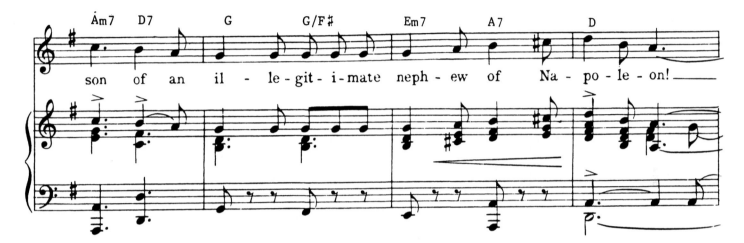

but the old sim - o - le - on!   I must know
(All to President) You so - and -

why   You cru - ci - fy   My na - tive
so!   We did - n't know   She had a

coun - try   With this ef - front' - ry
tie - up   So ver - y high - up!

To the il - le - git - i - mate daugh - ter of an
She's the il - le - git - i - mate daugh - ter of an

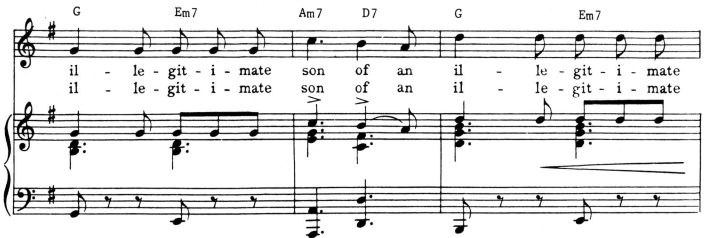

il - le - git - i -mate son of an il - le - git - i -mate

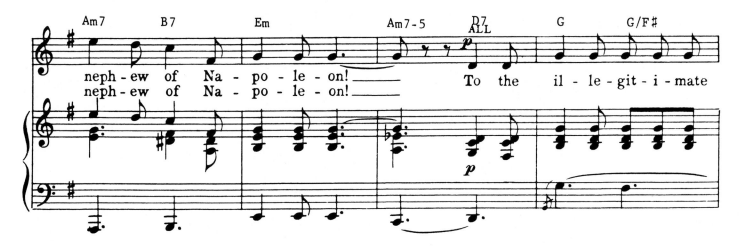

neph - ew of Na - po - le - on! _____ To the il - le - git - i -mate

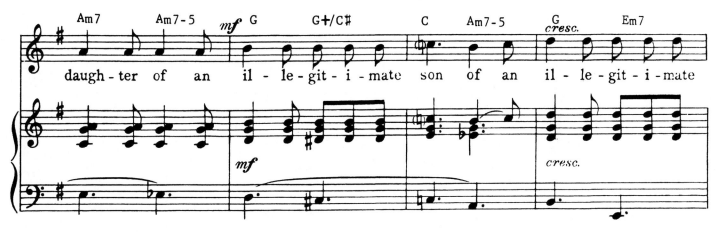

daugh - ter of an il - le - git - i -mate son of an il - le - git - i -mate

neph - ew of Na - po - le - on! She's the

The Illegitimate Daughter - 5 - 5

I'M A POACHED EGG

Music and Lyrics by
GEORGE GERSHWIN and IRA GERSHWIN

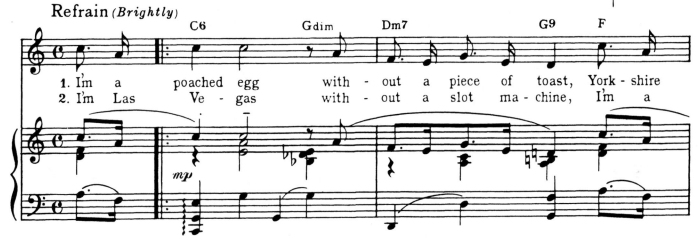

Refrain *(Brightly)*

1. I'm a poached egg with-out a piece of toast, York-shire
2. I'm Las Ve-gas with-out a slot ma-chine, I'm a

pud-ding with-out a beef to roast, I'm a haunt-ed house that
gyp-sy with-out a tam-bour-ine, I'm Na-po-le-on with-

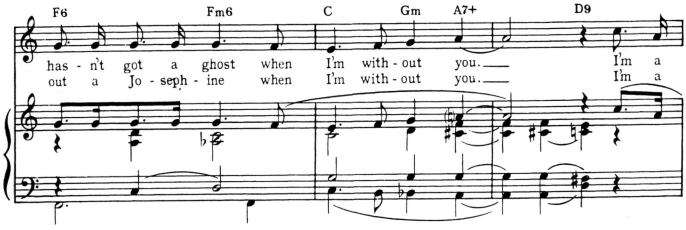

has-n't got a ghost when I'm with-out you.___ I'm a
out a Jo-seph-ine when I'm with-out you.___ I'm a

I'm a Poached Egg - 4 - 2

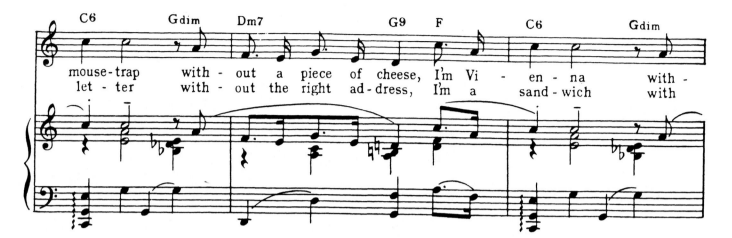

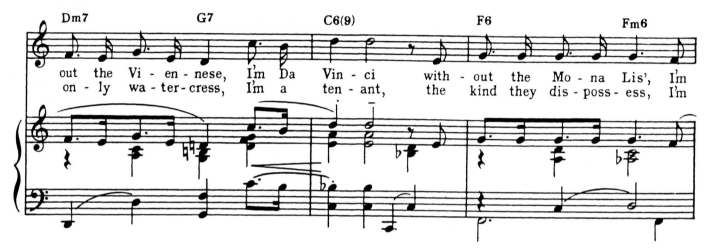

I'm a Poached Egg - 4 - 3

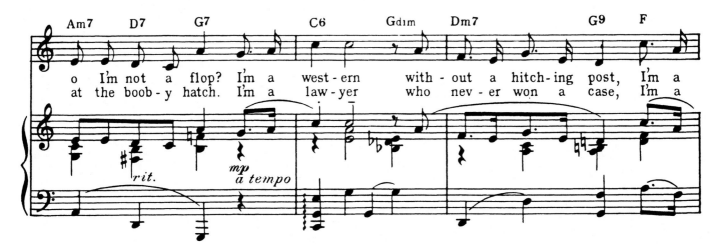

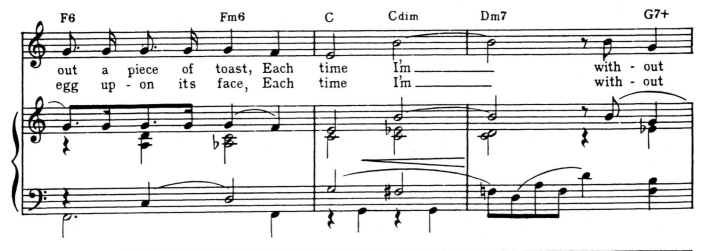

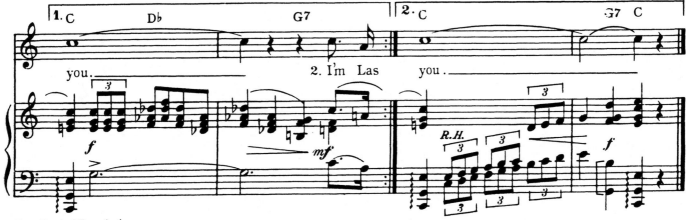

I'm a Poached Egg - 4 - 4

THE JOLLY TAR AND THE MILK MAID

Music and Lyrics by
GEORGE GERSHWIN and IRA GERSHWIN

Allegretto scherzando

VERSE

There was a Jol - ly Brit - ish Tar who
The Jol - ly Tar, he laughed a laugh. "Tis

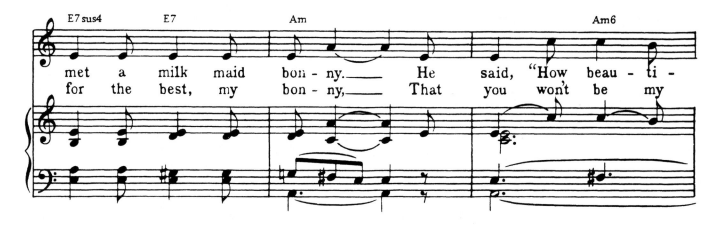

met a milk maid bon - ny.___ He said, "How beau - ti -
for the best, my bon - ny,___ That you won't be my

ful you are!" With a hey___ and a non - ny,___ With a
bet - ter half." With a hey___ and a non - ny,___ With a

The Jolly Tar and the Milk Maid - 4 - 1

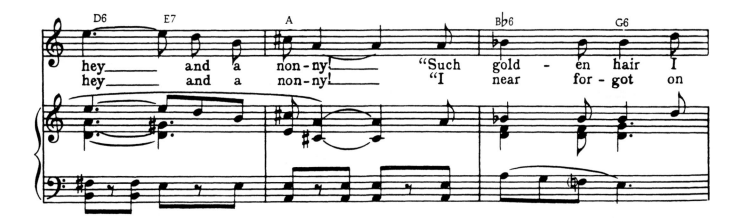

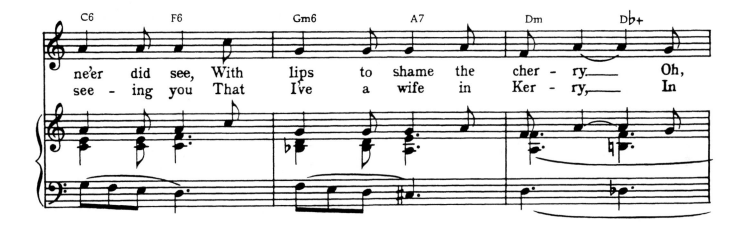

The Jolly Tar and the Milk Maid - 4 - 2

58

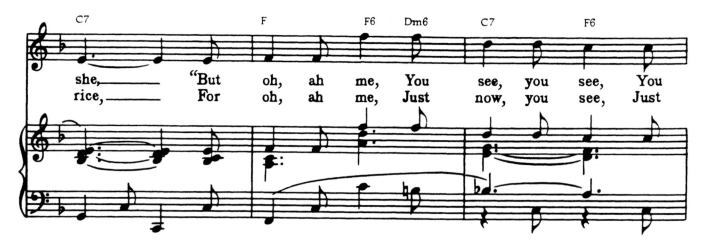

The Jolly Tar and the Milk Maid - 4 - 3

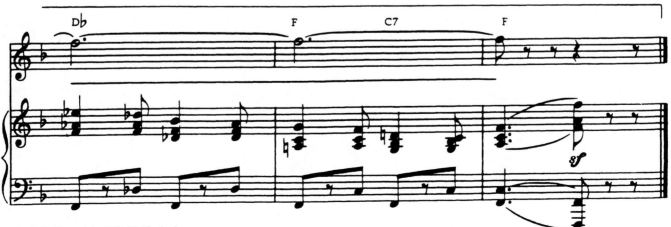

The Jolly Tar and the Milk Maid - 4 - 4

JUST ANOTHER RHUMBA

Music and Lyrics by
GEORGE GERSHWIN and IRA GERSHWIN

Just Another Rhumba - 8 - 1

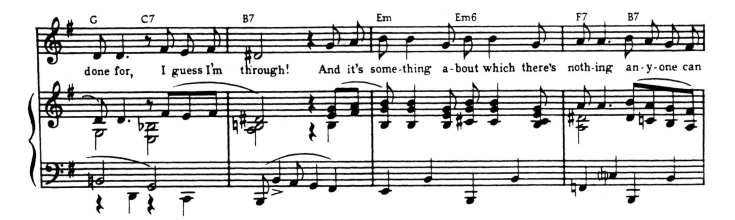

Just Another Rhumba - 8 - 2

64

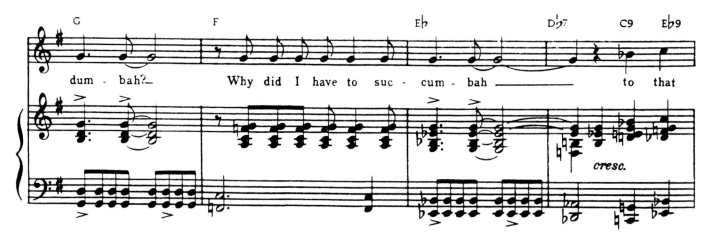

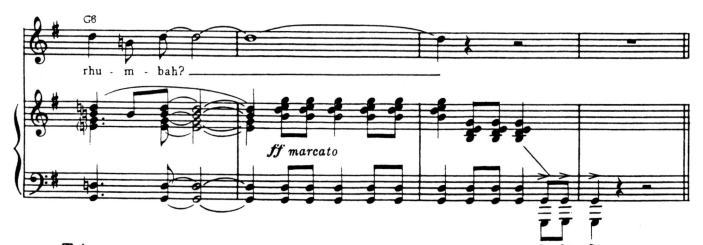

Trio

Just Another Rhumba - 8 - 5

Just Another Rhumba - 8 - 6

66

Just Another Rhumba - 8 - 7

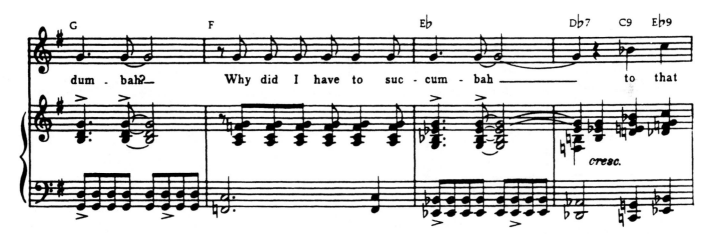

Just Another Rhumba - 8 - 8

THE LORELEI

Words and Music by
GEORGE GERSHWIN and IRA GERSHWIN

The Lorelei - 4 - 1

She cre-a-ted quite a stir And I want to be like her.

REFRAIN

I want to be like that gal on the riv-er, Who sang her

song to the ships pass-ing by; She had the goods and how she could de-

liv-er ___ The Lor-e-lei! ___ She used to love in a strange kind of

The Lorelei - 4 - 2

fash-ion,   With lots of hey! ho - de - ho! hi - de - hi!   And

I can guar-an-tee I'm full of pas - sion ____ Like the Lor - e - lei. ____

____   I'm treach-er-ous Ja!   Ja!   Oh, I just can't hold my -

self in check. I'm lech - er - ous Ja!   Ja!   I want to

bite my in - i - tials on a sail - or's neck! Each af - fair has a kick and a

wal - lop, For what they crave I can al - ways sup - ply I

want to be just like that oth - er trol - lop The Lor - e - lei! _____ I want to

Lor - e - lei! _____

The Lorelei - 4 - 4

MADEMOISELLE IN NEW ROCHELLE

Music and Lyrics by
GEORGE GERSHWIN and IRA GERSHWIN

Mademoiselle in New Rochelle - 4 - 1

Refrain Allegretto

Mademoiselle in New Rochelle - 4 - 2

74

75

Mademoiselle in New Rochelle - 4 - 4

MISCHA, JASCHA, TOSCHA, SASCHA

Music and Lyrics by
GEORGE GERSHWIN and
ARTHUR FRANCIS *(Ira Gershwin)*

MY COUSIN IN MILWAUKEE

Words and Music by
GEORGE GERSHWIN and IRA GERSHWIN

My Cousin in Milwaukee - 5 - 1

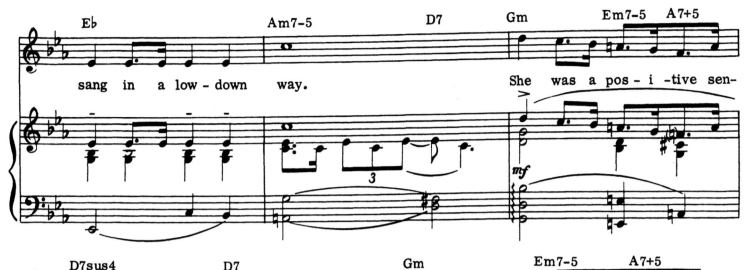

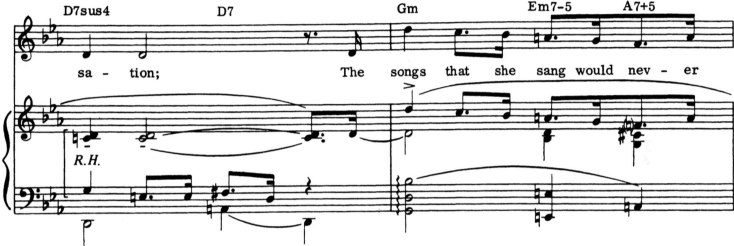

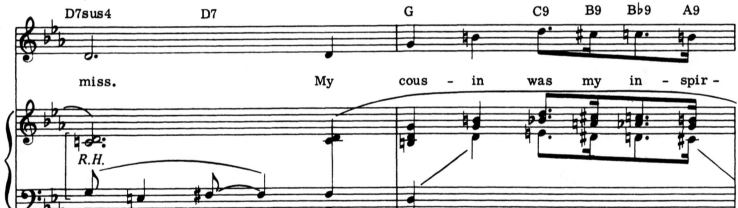

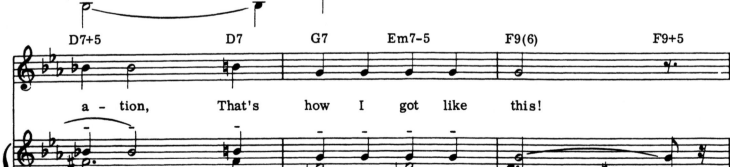

lot of sta - tic,_____ But makes your heart get ac - ro-bat - ic _____

Nine times out of ten._____ When

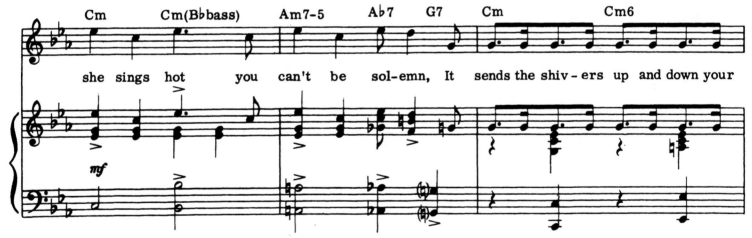

she sings hot you can't be sol-emn, It sends the shiv - ers up and down your

spin - al col-umn; When she sings blue, the men shout, "What stuff!

SO WHAT?

Music and Lyrics by
GEORGE GERSHWIN and IRA GERSHWIN

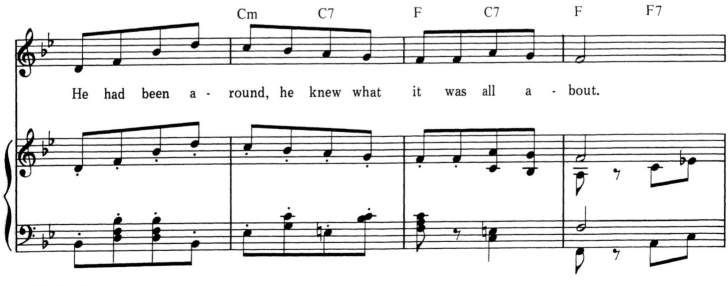

So What? - 5 - 1

When the rain would pat - ter, he'd say, "Does it mat - ter?"

And he'd have an - oth - er plate of sau - sa - ges and 'kraut. When

peo - ple told him of their trou - bles he would al - ways say, "So

well? So what? Per - haps to - mor - row is your luck - y day."

If you'll act as he did, noth-ing else is need - ed, and you'll be mer - ry as the month of May.____

Refrain

You sigh; so what? Soon you're laugh - ing.

So what? So you might as well be laugh - ing

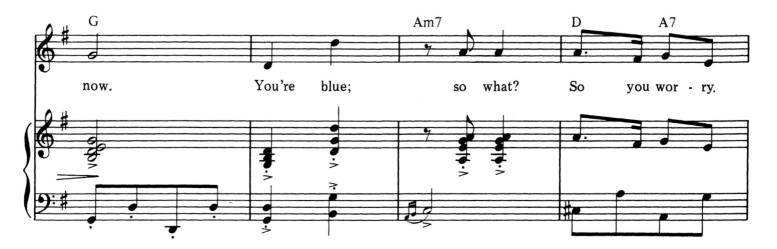

now. You're blue; so what? So you wor - ry.

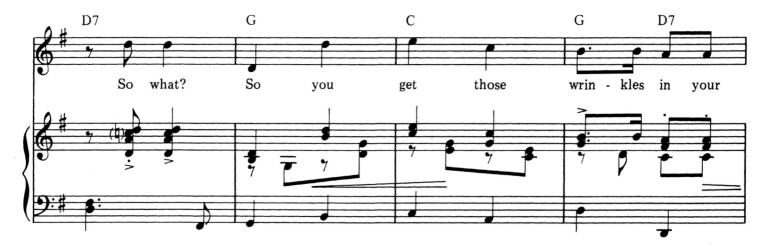

So what? So you get those wrin - kles in your

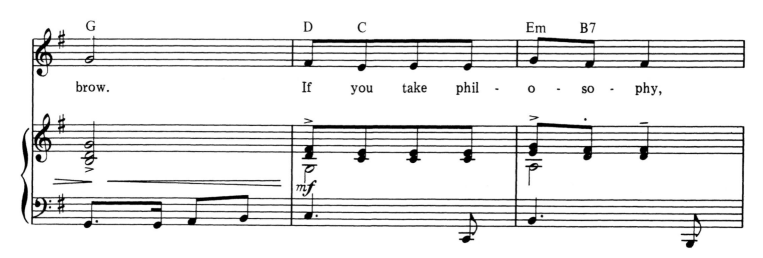

brow. If you take phil - o - so - phy,

just what do you find? Ev - 'ry rain - bow has a blue - bird

sil - ver - lined. You cry; so what?

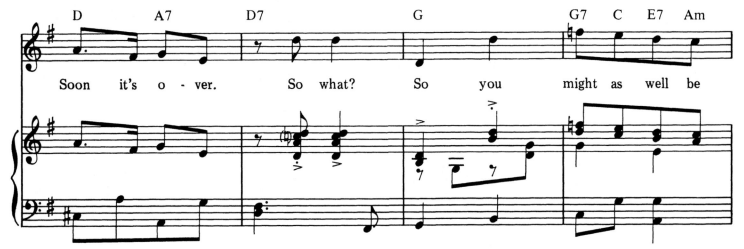

Soon it's o - ver. So what? So you might as well be

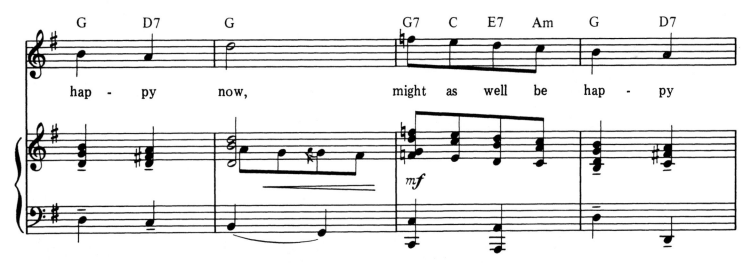

hap - py now, might as well be hap - py

1. now!

2. now! _____

NAUGHTY BABY

Music and Lyrics by
GEORGE GERSHWIN, IRA GERSHWIN
and DESMOND CARTER

Naughty Baby - 4 - 1

93

Naughty Baby - 4 - 4

ONE, TWO, THREE

Music and Lyrics by
GEORGE GERSHWIN and IRA GERSHWIN

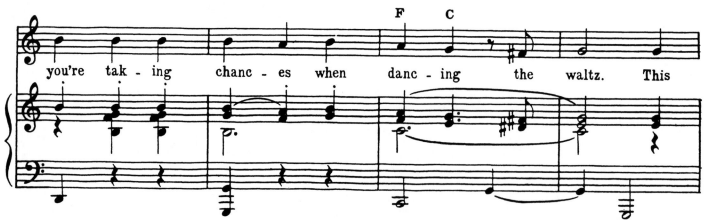

One, Two, Three - 4 - 1

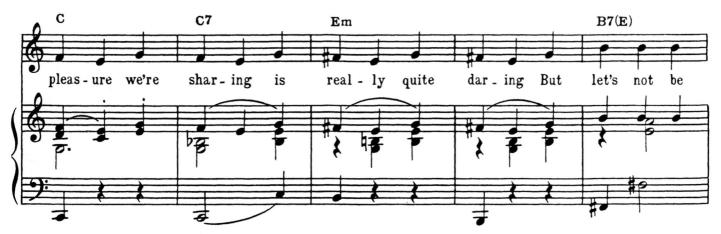

pleas - ure we're shar - ing is real - ly quite dar - ing But let's not be

car - ing till the band halts. If I had my way I'd en -

deav - or To keep waltz - ing for - ev - er.

One, two, three, One, two, three, One, two, three!

One, Two, Three - 4 - 4

THE SENATOR FROM MINNESOTA

Music and Lyrics by
GEORGE GERSHWIN and IRA GERSHWIN

The Senator From Minnesota - 4 - 1

coun - try thinks it's got de - pres - sion, Ha! ha! ha! Just

wait un - til we get in ses - sion, Ha! ha! ha! The

peo - ple want a lot of ac - tion, Ho! ho! ho! We're

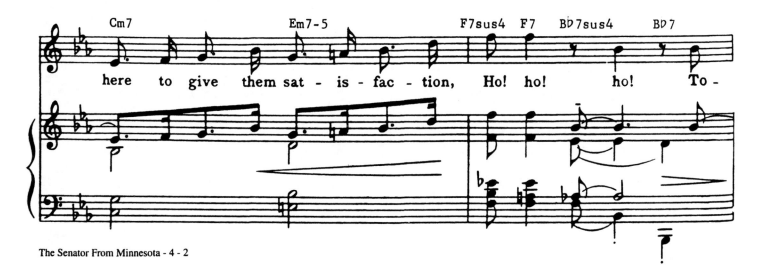

here to give them sat - is - fac - tion, Ho! ho! ho! To -

The Senator From Minnesota - 4 - 2

day is real-ly full of laugh-ter, Ha ha! ha! Com-

pared to what will fol-low af-ter, Ha ha! ha! There's

ac-tion ev-'ry min-ute when this hap-py group con-venes: To get

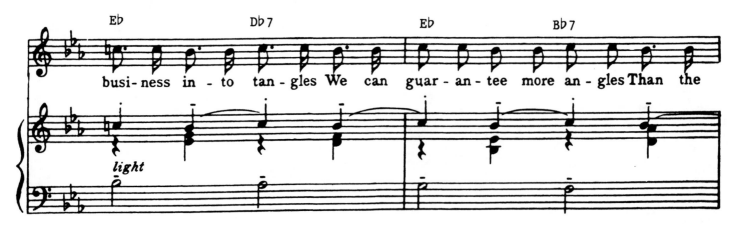

busi-ness in-to tan-gles We can guar-an-tee more an-gles Than the

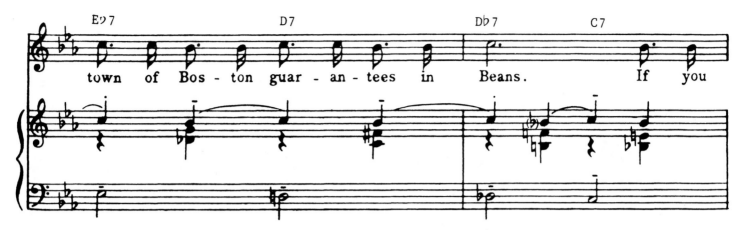

The Senator From Minnesota - 4 - 4

STIFF UPPER LIP

Music and Lyrics by
GEORGE GERSHWIN and IRA GERSHWIN

Moderato (with humor)

Verse:

What made good Queen Bess such a great suc - cess?

What made Well-ing - ton do what he did at Wa - ter - loo?

What makes ev - 'ry Eng - lish - man a fight - er through and through? It

Stiff Upper Lip - 4 - 1

THESE CHARMING PEOPLE

Music and Lyrics by
GEORGE GERSHWIN and IRA GERSHWIN

These Charming People - 4 - 1

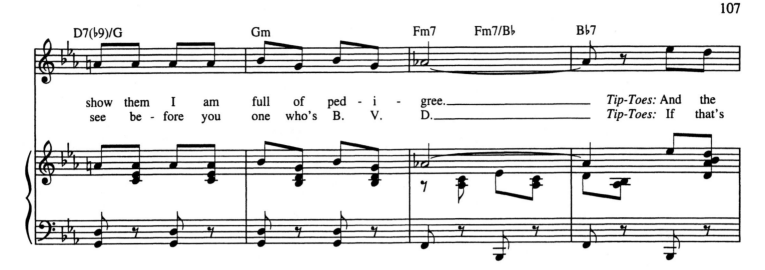

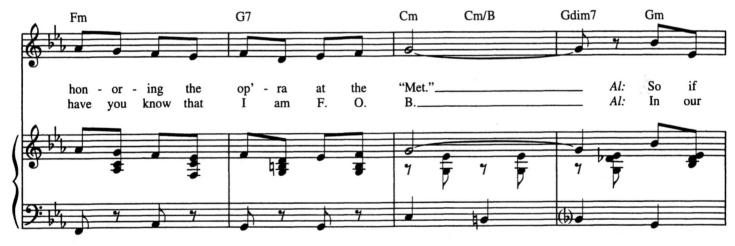

These Charming People - 4 - 2

UNION SQUARE

Music and Lyrics by
GEORGE GERSHWIN and IRA GERSHWIN

113

Union Square - 7 - 4

114

Union Square - 7 - 5